Original title:
Ocean Breezes and Coconut Trees

Copyright © 2025 Creative Arts Management OÜ
All rights reserved.

Author: William Hawthorne
ISBN HARDBACK: 978-1-80581-589-1
ISBN PAPERBACK: 978-1-80581-116-9
ISBN EBOOK: 978-1-80581-589-1

Whispering Winds of the Twilight Hour

Seagulls squawk as they swoop down,
Sandy toes leave prints all around.
A crab in a hat, feeling so grand,
Does the cha-cha, it's a hilarious stand.

Bikini tops start to shift and slide,
While jellyfish wiggle in the tide.
Someone just screamed at a splashing wave,
It's the best comedy, you just gotta rave.

Dreamscapes on Sunlit Retreats

Tanning oil, a slippery mess,
A seagull nabs my sandwich, I guess.
Laughter rolls like the rising foam,
As I chase the thief, my heart feels at home.

Beach balls fly high, make a grand show,
Tracking sand grains everywhere I go.
Someone's floatie just flipped on a ride,
And we all burst into fits, side by side.

Echoes of Laughter by the Water

Flip-flops slapping, what a ruckus,
Got splashed by a kid who's far too curious.
Sunburns and giggles, the perfect mix,
A crab in a shell, performing its tricks.

The sun is setting, oh what a sight,
As we dance with shadows, laughter takes flight.
An old man's story makes us all sway,
He lost a bet to a turtle today!

Midnight Serenades by the Shore

Under the stars, we sing and we sigh,
A fishy tale makes everyone cry.
Sandcastles crumble with each silly joke,
As waves join in, they laugh and provoke.

A mermaid appears, with a flip of her tail,
Says, 'Do you have snacks, or should I set sail?'
The night is young, and laughter's the theme,
Join in the fun, it's all a big dream.

Groves of Serenity Under the Sun

In paradise where laughter thrives,
A squirrel wears a cap and dives.
The coconuts chuckle, they know the score,
As beach-goers dance, calling for more.

A parrot sings in offbeat rhyme,
Calling out the wrong drink every time.
The sun's a clown, with shades and a grin,
While tourists trip over their flip-flops in.

Glimmers on Golden Waves

The waves are winking, playfully bright,
A fish flips over, giving a fright.
Seagulls steal fries with no hint of shame,
They wear tiny shades, all part of their game.

Sunbathers squabble, who's got the best tan?
While kids build castles with a sea-salt plan.
A crab in a bucket throws up a fuss,
"Excuse me, folks! You're blocking my bus!"

Afternoon Serenade by the Beach

With ukuleles strumming, folks sing along,
A cat in the sand thinks it's where it belongs.
The wind tickles cheeks, blowing hats in the air,
While dolphins leap high, without a single care.

A turtle in shades moves with style and grace,
While kids toss their snacks, thinking it's race.
The laughter erupts, a joyful parade,
In this light-hearted game, no sunblock was made!

Fronds Swaying to the Ocean's Tune

The breeze brings whispers, tickles our toes,
While tourists sip drinks with hilarious woes.
A waiter drops ice, a cascade so grand,
And laughter erupts like a band on the sand.

Palm leaves are gossiping, it's quite the affair,
As flip-flops go flying, like birds through the air.
Life's a grand circus, with clowns everywhere,
Each day's a new act, with joy to share!

Serenity of the Sunlit Retreat

Under bright rays, dreams take flight,
Sipping cold drinks; oh, what a sight!
Seagulls squawk, strutting their flair,
While sunburnt folks pull at their hair.

Flip-flops squeak with each goofy step,
Tanned strangers bust out their best rep.
Palm trees giggle at the scene,
As beach balls bounce, bright and keen.

Chasing Shadows on Sandy Pathways

Footprints left, a silly race,
As crabs scuttle, making their case.
Beach hats fly like kites in a jest,
Sand castles crumbling, they just won't rest.

The sun sets low, a golden glow,
Like a playful dog stealing the show.
Laughter echoes, filling the air,
With each slip and trip, who'll take the dare?

Tales carried by the Wind

Whispers of laughter ride the breeze,
As life's a joke beneath the trees.
Waves come crashing with a splashy cheer,
While surfboards wobble, never appear.

Stories float like jellyfish, bright,
Of tan lines and sunscreen, sheer delight.
The wind tells tales of comical fails,
In this funny land where humor prevails.

The Dance of Fronds and Foam

Fronds sway gently, in rhythm they play,
A silly dance that steals the day.
Foamy waves giggle, tickling toes,
As laughter drowns all worry, it flows.

Coconuts cheer, as they silently shake,
In the warm sun, for goodness' sake!
With ice cream cones melting away,
Here's a toast to the funny ballet!

Sandy Shores and Skylit Dreams

The grains of sand, they tickle my feet,
I dance around, it's quite the treat!
A seagull squawks, it steals my fries,
I can't help but laugh, as my stomach sighs.

With sun hats flying in the light breeze,
I wave to the crabs, the little tease.
My sunscreen's a blob, just like my face,
At this wacky beach, I've found my place.

Corals in the Warm Embrace

Fish wear shades, they look so cool,
I make a splash, but I feel like a fool.
The coral giggles with colors bright,
And I can't tell if it's day or night.

Blowing bubbles and feeling free,
A dolphin joins, he laughs at me.
With seashells stacked like wobbly towers,
I'm the king of sand, for a few short hours.

A Symphony of Nature's Breath

Palm trees sway in a bizarre jig,
I join in, looking quite the big wig.
Each gust of wind sings a silly song,
I dance like a fool, but I can't go wrong.

The waves crash down, they're giggling loud,
I try to surf, yet I'm more cowed.
A crab flicks sand, it's quite the treat,
As I tumble backward, I land on my seat.

Lullabies of the Coastal Winds

Napping on rocks with a crabby friend,
He tells me tales, they never end.
As seagulls swoop, they laugh and tease,
I wake up just in time to sneeze!

The sunset paints the sky in jest,
I jerk awake, it's quite the test.
With laughter echoing through the air,
A goofy grin, without a care.

Nature's Breath and Tropical Tangles

The sunbeams dance on waves so bright,
Where crabs in disco move left and right,
A parrot squawks a tune so odd,
While seagulls plot a beachside fraud.

In the shade, a monkey starts to sway,
Stealing snacks, and laughing all the way,
Coconuts drop like thunderous applause,
As beachgoers dodge them with comic jaws.

Serene Shores and Forgotten Tales.

A turtle named Fred wore stylish shades,
While a jellyfish dropped in mermaid parades,
Flip-flops squeak and kids chase their dreams,
Sandcastle battles burst at the seams.

Old fishermen boast with a crooked grin,
Tall tales of fish, where do we begin?
The octopus shyly waves from his lair,
Wishing for snacks, not a fishy affair.

Whispers of the Tidal Winds

The breezes chatter with a youthful cheer,
As beach balls bounce and cold drinks appear,
A squirrel in a hat takes all the snacks,
Claiming the best spot, with no looking back.

Surfers glide like they own the sea,
But wipeouts turn into slapstick glee,
The tide rolls in with a splash and a sigh,
While seahorses giggle as dolphins fly by.

Palms in the Gentle Zephyr

The palm trees wiggle, wearing leafy bling,
As wind whispers softly, in gale-like swing,
A crab plays hide and seek with a star,
While embracing the sunlight near and far.

Cocktails clink with a festive jingle,
Mermaids laugh, where they dance and mingle,
In this quirky realm, where fun never sleeps,
The sand tickles toes, as the laughter leaps.

Cascading Dreams Under Swaying Fronds

In the sun, I waddle with glee,
A seagull snickers at me.
I trip on my flip-flops' lace,
Landing right on my face!

The palmtree leans down to tease,
Pretending it wants to sneeze.
Dancing leaves start to sway,
I join, hip-shaking all day!

Nature's Rhythm and Coastal Calm

The crabs throw a seaside rave,
All the locals watch and brave.
Dressed in shells, on the sand they prance,
Performing their best crustacean dance.

The waves are like a playful pup,
Chasing me with a gentle sup.
I leap and squeal, oh what a sight,
As the surf gives me a sloppy bite!

The Lure of Sun and Sea

A clam tried to sell me a pearl,
But it was made out of swirl!
It giggled and said, 'Take a chance!,'
As I slipped and fell in a trance.

A beach ball bounced, a rogue balloon,
Skimming the sand like a cartoon.
I chased it down, my fighting pride,
Barefoot and flopping, where'd it hide?

Fragrant Breezes of Eden's Embrace

The mangoes act like they know best,
Competing for who'll be the zest.
I tried to eat one, what a mess,
With sticky hands, I must confess!

A tow-headed child flies by with glee,
Tripped on his own, oh dear, oh me!
While laughing, he lands in the sand,
Calling for help but looking so grand!

Cool Caresses of Island Air

The wind tickles me as I walk,
It whispers secrets, makes me squawk.
The seagulls giggle, dive with grace,
As I trip on sand, fall on my face.

Palm trees sway, a dance routine,
They wave at sun, and look so keen.
I wave back, but they're too tall,
I swear they're stirring up a squall!

Here comes a breeze, just like a tease,
It lifts my hat, steals my keys.
Laughter echoes, the waves applaud,
As seashells giggle at my façade.

With every gust, a playful shove,
The sun shines bright, I'm feeling love.
Sand between my toes, what a mess,
But oh, this chaos? I must confess!

Horizons Infinite and Inviting

The horizon meets the sky's big grin,
It winks at boats that bob and spin.
Seagulls parade, good moods abound,
While I just trip on this loose ground.

The sun flips pancakes, golden and round,
While fish throw parties, splash all around.
I wave to clouds, they puff and float,
Then laugh as I try to balance a boat.

The beach ball rolls, makes a grand escape,
It bounces away, oh what a shape!
Kids chase after, laughter so sweet,
While I sip lemonade, feeling the heat.

With each wave's laugh, the world gets bright,
A search for sunscreen, first in the light.
Horizons flirt, at the edge of sway,
In this crazy fun, I wish to stay!

Secrets Hidden in Tidal Pools

In little pools, where treasures hide,
Crabs play poker, my shoes beside.
Starfish tell tales, they wink at me,
While seashells sing in harmony.

Seaweed dances, quite the surprise,
It wraps my leg, oh what a prize!
Laughter bubbles, tidal waves sway,
As fish put on shows, wild and play.

A lonely conch plays a sad tune,
While I watch jellyfish float past the moon.
But wait! A dog leaps, slips on the sand,
Making waves with a pup's quick hand.

Secrets unfold beneath the sun's peak,
Where laughter and splashes play hide and seek.
In these tiny worlds, joy takes flight,
Oh, tidal pools, you're such a delight!

Light Play on the Water's Surface

The sun dances on waves, what a sight,
It jiggles and wiggles with sheer delight.
I try to catch it with my red cup,
But splash! Oh no! My drink's all up!

Fish play tag 'neath the shimmering glow,
While I sip slowly, taking it slow.
Laughter erupts from the small shore crew,
As I get splashed with a wave or two.

Paddle boards glide like big, silly ducks,
While they dodge swimmers and all of their clucks.
The sun's glowing face teases my gaze,
As I trip again in this watery maze.

Oh, light on the waves, you're a charming jest,
Turning simple moments into the best.
With each sparkle, a chuckle I feel,
This funny dance, oh, how surreal!

Murmurs of the Surf at Twilight

The seagulls squawk, a comical jest,
Chasing each other like they're on a quest.
One steals a chip from a tourist's snack,
The beach is a circus, a hilarious act.

Sunset spills gold on the sandy shore,
An old man slips, then dances some more.
His hat's blown away, a kite on the run,
Laughter erupts, oh, what silly fun!

Sandcastles rise, then get washed away,
Kids giggle loud, "It's just a sea spray!"
A crab plays tag with a shoe left behind,
While a toddler thinks it's his new friend, unkind.

As twilight beckons, promises repeat,
The moon winks down, oh, isn't it sweet?
The waves whisper secrets, a soft, silly tune,
Dancing and laughing beneath the big moon.

Nature's Palette of Aqua and Green

By the shore, a pickle jar floats by,
Filled with treasures, oh my, oh my!
The kids dive in, thinking it's gold,
But find just seaweed and stories retold.

A parrot squawks, with a voice so loud,
"Would you like a cracker?" he speaks to the crowd.
He steals their snacks, a crafty little thief,
Everyone chuckles, beneath their disbelief.

The sun wears shades, strutting its rays,
While flip-flops dance on their sunny ballet.
A beach ball bounces, a dog thinks it's lunch,
The laughter grows louder, a silly brunch.

With every splash, joy takes flight,
The day winds down, but oh, what a sight!
As tides ebb back, they leave sun-kissed glee,
Nature paints smiles, from sea to sea.

Lush Tales of Coastal Lullabies

Beneath the palms, a hammock swings,
Catching dreams from the laughter it brings.
A crab throws shade at a beach chair snoozer,
While pelicans play, a comedy chooser.

Children twirl like they're riding the breeze,
Falling in sand, but they laugh with ease.
"Watch my somersault!" one proudly proclaims,
Then faces the surf—well, the joke's on the game.

Starfish watching with arms splayed wide,
Grinning at tourists who run with pride.
With sunscreen smeared, looking quite a sight,
They frolic and giggle as day turns to night.

The stars join the fest, twinkling as they sway,
To the rhythm of waves, in their own playful way.
Nature hums softly, stories so funny,
As the world settles down, bathed in moon's honey.

Waves of Memory and Time

A floatie drifts, shaped like a whale,
Kids hop on board, though some may fail.
They giggle and splash in a wobbly race,
While onlookers laugh, not a care on their face.

The tides recall tales of days gone past,
Of sandy mishaps that always last.
Grandpa lost a shoe in a funny old dive,
Now it's a legend that keeps laughter alive.

Turtles in shades chill out on a rock,
While jellyfish dance, doing the clock.
With a wink and a wave, they bid us goodnight,
To the sounds of the surf, under stars shining bright.

Mirth in the sea salt, joy in the spray,
Time laughs along as the sun fades away.
Each wave brings a chuckle, a fun little rhyme,
Echoing memories, unfurling through time.

The Stillness Between Tides

Waves flop and flop, but why do they play?
The fish wear sunglasses, it's quite the display.
Seagulls gossip loud, while crabs hold a dance,
In this sandy soirée, everyone takes a chance.

Flip-flops get lost, while the towels do fight,
A sunscreen mishap, oh what a sight!
Shells swirl like hats, on each little head,
Even the sandflowers giggle instead.

Jumping in puddles of brine and of fun,
The sun's on a mission, oh isn't it done?
Kids with ice cream, drippy and sweet,
Chasing down laughter, a tropical treat.

Breezes that Carry Dreams

Whispers of whims swipe the hair from my face,
Where dreams catch a lift at a comical pace.
Sailboats like ducks, bobbing all around,
With each gust of giggles, they lose their way found.

The hammock's a rocket, swinging off the ground,
A flamingo joins in with a silly sound.
Breezes like jesters perform their own plots,
Telling tales of seaweed and fish that wear spots.

The clouds have a party, a fluffy brigade,
Where shadows slip in for a wobbly parade.
Kites tangled in laughter, with strings interlaced,
Nature's own humor, a delightful embrace.

Under the Shade of Swaying Palms

Beneath leafy umbrellas, we sip from our cups,
While ants wear tuxedos and join us for ups.
Sipping our coconuts with straws made of grass,
Even the lizards are sporting some sass.

Chairs dance around in this breeze-swayed affair,
The sunlight is giggling, with warmth it will share.
A parrot cracks jokes that are totally nuts,
While we throw our worries to the wiggly guts.

Cool mist of the shade feels just like a cheer,
As sunlight and laughter birth memories here.
Giggling shells whisper of secrets so bright,
Creating our stories from morning to night.

Tropical Echoes of Laughter

Echoes of chuckles bounce off the blue,
As snappy fish dive, making a hullabaloo.
Pelicans ponder their next meal of choice,
While the waves giggle softly, they have quite the voice.

The crabs are a band, with shells as their drums,
Playing tunes that attract all the happy little chums.
Wild parties of seaweed celebrate with a thud,
Partying in nooks, making the ocean a stud.

Blowing up bubbles, like balloons in the sky,
The world spins a tale, where we simply must try.
Laughter and sunlight, they twirl hand in hand,
In a world full of dreams, oh isn't it grand?

Driftwood Stories Beneath the Skies

Driftwood dreams float on so high,
Seagulls gossip as they fly.
A crab wears sunglasses, quite absurd,
While fish debate the latest word.

Beach towels clash like rival teams,
Sandy sandwiches fill our dreams.
Flip-flops squeak, a silly sound,
As laughter dances all around.

Under a sun that likes to bake,
A jellyfish pulls its best prank shake.
With each wave, a new tale spun,
Who knew such fun could weigh a ton?

Serenity Woven in Green and Blue

Palm fronds sway with a friendly tease,
Whispers of ants parade with ease.
A turtle sunbathes, takes its time,
While crickets chirp their own sweet rhyme.

Waves roll in with a playful plop,
While beach balls bounce and never stop.
A seahorse wearing a tiny hat,
Ignores the gossip, what of that?

Beneath this sky with hues so bright,
A dolphin jokes—'I'll take a flight!'
We giggle at fish in a school,
They swim in style like they're so cool.

Laughter Beneath the Coconut Canopy

Underneath leaves of emerald hue,
A bird sings of secrets, something new.
A monkey swinging with style and flair,
Steals a snack with nary a care.

Just one sip from the coconut top,
Will make your worries come to a stop.
And crabs will dance with clumsy feet,
As mermaids giggle, oh, how sweet!

Sunscreen splatters like paint on a wall,
While kids make castles that rise and fall.
With every splash, a story told,
We wave to the sun, feeling quite bold.

Shores adorned with Nature's Lace

Seashells gossip, oh what a sound,
They tell of the wonders they've found.
A sandcastle brigade stands so proud,
While waves applaud, cheering out loud.

Crabs in a hurry, they dance on the sand,
Chasing their dreams in friendship's band.
A fish in a tuxedo passes by,
Winked at a starfish, oh my, oh my!

With every breeze, the tale unfolds,
Of laughter and joy worth more than gold.
So we gather, and with friends we play,
In this quirky paradise, we'll always stay.

Lullabies in the Shade

Underneath the palm leaves sway,
A crab sings songs to save the day.
The sand's a blanket, soft and fine,
But not for naps, it's snack time, dine!

Seagulls giggle while they dive,
Chasing flip-flops, they arrive.
With sunburned noses and frozen treats,
We dance like fish on silly feats.

Waves Crashing on Wanderlust

The surfboard's waiting, it's a sight,
But first, I need to take a bite.
A splashy dive? Not quite my skill,
I'd rather float and swig this swill!

With friends who laugh, we can't be still,
Caught in a wave that gives a thrill.
But there's a lobster who steals my hat,
And now I'm really getting flat!

Shades of Serenity

With sunglasses slipped upon my face,
I ponder life at a leisurely pace.
A sea turtle winks, I swear he's wise,
Playing peek-a-boo with beachy skies.

We sip on drinks that giggle and fizz,
My hat flies off, but hey, who is?
The waves invited us to play,
But my sandwich goes astray!

Coconut Skies and Sandy Feet

Each coconut drops with a plop and a smile,
While seagulls steal fries, oh what a style!
Sunshine melts ice cream, sticky and sweet,
I dance with my sandals, flapping my feet.

Footprints lead nowhere, just like my goals,
I laugh at the tide as it tickles my soles.
In this paradise, so wild and free,
I'm just a beach bum, filled with glee!

Whispers of the Tidal Winds

Seagulls squawk with glee, hard to ignore,
As fish wear sunglasses, with fins galore.
The tide tells secrets, but I'm not sure,
If it's a fish tale or just a seagull's snore.

Waves dance a jig, they really rock,
Clams do the salsa, it's quite the shock.
I brought my surfboard, but it's a block,
Next time I'll stick to just beachside mock!

The salty spritz tickles my nose,
Jellyfish prance, wearing big bows.
Seashells giggle, who knows how it goes,
As crabs throw a party, in tiny clothes.

Flip-flops clatter on the sandy plot,
With each goofy wave and each silly trot.
Mermaids take selfies, they hit the spot,
While I just trip, and fall with a splot.

Swaying Palms at Dusk

Palms sway in rhythm, like they're in a trance,
Cocktails in coconuts, let's take a chance.
The wind joins the party, it'll make you prance,
While crabs try their luck in a crabby dance.

A squirrel in shades claims the best seat,
As sun drops low, it can't be beat.
With a wink, he says, "Feel that heat!"
Bikini-clad ladies can't lose their feat.

Bananas on boats giggle as they float,
Riding the waves in a goofy boat.
I try to join, but end up like a goat,
With splashes abound, oh what a remote!

Everyone watches the sunset glow,
While parrot jokes fly, "Did you hear the show?"
Cracking up laughter, like waves in tow,
This silly escape is the best way to flow.

Saltwater Serenade

Sandcastles crumble as we cheer,
The tide comes in, our lunch draws near.
Seashells start singing, oh so clear,
As fish in tuxedos swim with a leer.

The sponge in my bag is quite a prank,
The seagulls revolt with a fishy shank.
But we all just laugh, thanks to our crank,
And the ocean's game is worth the rank.

The sunset glows like a big piece of toast,
As jellyfish float, claiming they're the host.
They toss seaweed, which most love to roast,
While dolphins jump in with a flip and boast.

Laughter erupts with each salty wave,
We call it a day; oh, how we behave!
With memories made, like treasures we save,
Under the sky, feeling quite brave.

Echoes of the Surfing Shore

Surfboards crash, the sound is quite bold,
But I fall right off, truth be told.
Waves are my friends, though rather cold,
Yet they giggle softly, as stories unfold.

The dolphins tease from their ocean cove,
With flips and spins, oh how they shove!
A mermaid yells, "Come join the grove!"
While I just splash, feeling far from a dove.

The beach party starts with a blur and a sway,
Oh, to be cool is the theme of the day.
I lose my flip-flop and shout in dismay,
As crabs laugh out loud, "Just dance anyway!"

As night rolls in, the stars start to twinkle,
The seaweed dons hats, makes us all crinkle.
With laughter and joy, our hearts all twinkle,
Among whispering waves, we are all sprinkles.

Harmony Among the Fronds

When palm trees sway with glee,
They tickle the sea's big toe.
Seagulls squawk their lovely song,
As crabs dance in a sandy show.

Laughter floats on salty air,
While starfish juggle shells with flair.
The sun wears shades, a funny sight,
As flip-flops take a daring flight.

Coconuts giggle high above,
While shells gossip, full of love.
Oh, the joy that fills the bay,
Where clams and fish just want to play.

With every breeze that sweeps on by,
The seaweed waves, oh me, oh my!
A beach ball bounces off a whale,
And laughter echoes, loud and frail.

Sunset Moods and Misty Roots

The sky turns pink, a painter's dream,
As crabs make plans to plot and scheme.
Glowworms dance in evening light,
While fish tell tales of silly fright.

Tidal pools hold secrets deep,
As starfish study, just to peep.
Octopuses wear hats so grand,
And surfboards ride the grainy sand.

A dolphin mimics all our moves,
While pelicans show off their grooves.
Even sunsets can crack a joke,
With every wave, a new poke.

The palm trees nod, they understand,
As breezy whispers sweep the land.
And when the night begins to hum,
We laugh at sea, oh what a fun!

Gentle Tides and Horizon's Glow

With every wave, a splash of glee,
The fish all sing, "Come dance with me!"
Nautical nonsense fills the air,
As gulls play tag without a care.

Surfboards wobble in a line,
As sunburnt tourists drink their wine.
The tide rolls in with cheeky grins,
While jellyfish dance, wearing fins.

Sandcastles rise, then take a fall,
As everyone rushes for the ball.
The seagulls cackle, taking bets,
While beach umbrellas start to set.

When twilight glows with hints of gold,
The laughter rings, and stories told.
In this silly world, we find our place,
Where fun is found in every space.

Island Haze and Dreaming Waves

The mangoes toss, a fruity mess,
As island dogs wear fancy dress.
We dance around a coconut,
While lazy lizards giggle, "What?"

Sandy toes and giggly groups,
The tides recite the silliest loops.
Anemones wave and wink with glee,
As we sip drinks from a fruit tree.

Fishermen tell of fish so grand,
Yet they're no bigger than a hand.
The shores are lined with goofy sights,
As laughter carries through the nights.

With every wave, the secrets spill,
The salty air gives quite a thrill.
In this haze of sun and fun,
Life's a game, and we have won.

Ocean-Salted Breezes at Dusk

The seagulls squawk, they steal my fries,
I glare at them with blazing eyes.
A wave rolls in, it hugs my feet,
I laugh and dance to my own beat.

A crab scuttles, quite the sight,
He thinks he's fierce, but he's a fright.
I wave to fish, they swim away,
Guess they won't join my seafood play.

The sun dips low, a fruity drink,
Sipped through a straw, I start to think.
My friends all tease, my hair's a mess,
But I'm the queen of this sandy dress.

With laughter loud, the stars appear,
The night is young, let's all give cheer!
We'll toast to tides and silly games,
And make it fun with wacky names.

Tales of the Warm, Embracing Breeze

The warm wind whispers in my ear,
It tells me jokes and brings good cheer.
I trip on flip-flops, what a sight,
My friends all laugh, it's pure delight.

A parrot squawks, he's got some sass,
He mimics me as I trip and pass.
We chase our hats, lost in the sun,
A game of tag? Oh, this is fun!

The palm trees sway, they dance so free,
I wish I could, but I'm too clumsy.
With coconut snacks, we munch and tease,
This day is perfect for laughs and ease.

As sunset dims, we play charades,
Pretend to surf on imaginary waves.
The stars wink down, and laughter's loud,
Another night, and we are proud!

Hushed Secrets of the Twilight Coast

The tide rolls in with quiet grace,
While I just try to find my place.
I slip and slide in my wet shoes,
And giggle at my silly moves.

A whispering breeze with secrets told,
It swirls my hair, a golden mold.
A sea sponge floats by, quite the show,
I poke it gently, 'What do you know?'

The twilight glows, the crickets sing,
I dance like no one's watching, spring.
A turtle lumbers, head held high,
The keenest party-goer's alibi!

Yet in the dusk, there's laughter free,
As we share stories by the sea.
With giggles light, we won't depart,
These hushed moments steal my heart.

Golden Dreams Under Tropical Skies

Under skies so blue and bright,
I launched my dreams, gave them a flight.
But here comes a wave, to my surprise,
It toppled me, oh what a rise!

A hermit crab, with tiny shell,
Winks at me, as if to yell.
I pick him up, he gives a frown,
I swear he thinks I'm quite the clown.

The pineapple drinks are cold and sweet,
They slip right down, oh what a treat.
We laugh and joke, the day's not through,
Just here for fun, with skies so blue!

As twilight falls, we dance in glee,
The stars above, our company.
We toast our dreams, with laughter shared,
In this paradise, we're unprepared!

Tropical Embrace

On sandy shores where seagulls squawk,
I tried to surf but fell like a rock.
My board went left, I went to the right,
It's a laughing matter, what a sight!

Beneath the sun, I sip my drink,
A squirrel stole it, quick as a blink.
He danced away with my fruity prize,
While I just stood there, wide-eyed and surprised.

In flip-flops that squeak with every step,
I chased that critter, but he was adept.
He waved goodbye with a cheeky grin,
As I plopped down, dusting off my chin.

Dance of the Green Fronds

The leaves, they shimmy in the breeze,
Like disco dancers, aiming to please.
I twirl around, give it my best,
But trip on roots, oh what a jest!

A coconut drops with a thud and a crack,
I dodge it fast, but then I lack.
Trying to show off my fancy move,
I end up stuck in a move-less groove.

Laughter echoes from the palm tree crew,
They all take bets on what I'll do.
With limbs a-tangled, I start to sway,
Promised I'm graceful, another day!

Breezy Shores and Warm Embrace

A crab approaches with a sidestep dance,
I thought I'd join, just take a chance.
But he scuttled off with a sideways stare,
My best moves met with utter despair.

The salty air plays tricks on my hair,
It sticks and twirls, an unkempt affair.
I laugh at myself, a wild-haired clown,
In this beautiful place, I still wear a crown.

Seagulls caw above while I try to pose,
But my balance falters, and down I goes.
It's a tumble of laughter, rolling in sand,
In nature's circus, I'm part of the band.

Velvet Skies

The sunset paints the sky like a show,
But I missed the shot, oh no, oh no!
My phone fell in the drink, a splash and a flop,
It floated away like a pop star's prop!

Stars emerge, and fireflies ignite,
I try to catch one, but that's not quite right.
I stumble and fumble, with laughter I see,
The silly glowbugs just laugh at me!

As night falls gentle, I trip on a wave,
In this world, it's fun I crave.
I dance with the shadows, a goofy ballet,
And in the starry brightness, I laugh all the way.

Gentle Waves

In rippling shallows, I try to splash,
But misjudge the currents, oh what a crash!
Flippers flailing, my dignity lost,
The seabirds chuckle, I'm their very own cost.

A beach ball rolls past, I go for the score,
Then slip on a shell, no grace anymore.
With laughter untamed, the sun shakes its head,
While I pick myself up, and pretend I'm not red.

The gentle waves tease, they tickle my toes,
As I wobble around like a duck in repose.
In silly antics, joy takes the lead,
On this sandy stage, all we need is to be freed.

A Symphony of Salty Air

The seagulls squawk a silly song,
As I trip over my flip-flops long.
Crabs march sideways with a hasty dance,
While sunscreen leaves me in a greasy trance.

A dolphin leaps, a fishy surprise,
I thought it winked, those sparkling eyes.
My beach ball floats like a runaway kite,
Spotting a sandcastle, oh, what a sight!

The salty wind plays with my hair,
And my sandwich flies—I'm in despair.
Sunbathers laugh as they watch me chase,
A seagull munching on my lunch's base.

With laughter ringing beneath the sun,
I learn beach life can be quite a pun.
So grab your shades and dance in the spray,
Let's roll with the waves, come what may!

Sunlit Shores and Swaying Lullabies

A turtle wore my sunglasses right,
He waddled by, what a comical sight.
Nearby a child's running, lost in a race,
He collides with a sandpile—that's not his place!

The sun is hot, but I've got an idea,
I'll make a hat from my watermelon sphere.
But when I try, it rolls off my head,
And now I have juice, not much instead!

Beach umbrellas wave like flags in a storm,
As I sip my drink, feeling rather warm.
A crab tries to dance on my sandy chair,
To be honest, he's giving it quite a scare!

The waves whisper secrets, oh so sweet,
While I giggle at friends with sandy feet.
Let's gather shells, or maybe some laughs,
There's treasure in joy—just look at the staffs!

The Breeze's Gentle Caress

Under the shade, I take a seat,
With sticky fingers from a treat.
The breeze flirts like a cheeky muse,
Making my hat dance, I just can't snooze!

I toss my chips, and oh, what luck,
A flock of pigeons—my snack they pluck!
I try to run, reclaim what's mine,
But instead I trip, I have no spine!

A surfboard waits, a trusty steed,
But I've got balance that I don't need.
Upon the waves, I flop and flail,
While onlookers laugh—what a majestic fail!

But laughter's the pearl in this sunny sea,
As I wipe the salt from my cheek, whee!
So here's to the fun, and the beachy spree,
With twirls and swirls, oh let it be!

Warm Winds and Island Dreams

In the warm glow, a hammock swings,
My drink's half empty, but the fun it brings!
As I lay back, worries drift away,
A nap might ruin this perfect day.

A dog leaps by, steals my flip-flop—hey!
While I chase him down, I look quite the sway.
Later, we build a fort made of sand,
That collapses with laughter, oh isn't it grand?

The tide rolls in, like a mischievous friend,
Taking back toys that I didn't intend.
I'm left with shells, and twinkling eyes,
As the sun dips low, lighting up the skies.

So raise a toast to the joys we seek,
With giggles and glee, no time for bleak.
Together we dance on this sandy scene,
In a world full of wonder, where we laugh, yell, and glean!

Sun-Kissed Reflections of the Sea

The sun shines bright with a cheeky grin,
As seagulls squawk and dive right in.
The beach ball rolls, oh what a chase,
While sunscreen's smeared all over the face.

Waves are dancing, making a splash,
A crab in a hurry—oh, what a dash!
Flip-flops flying, laughter in the air,
The tide comes in with a mischievous flare.

A Canopy of Night Stars

Under the glow of a silver spoon,
We roast marshmallows to the tune.
The stars above start to giggle and sway,
As I trip on my toes, what a folly display!

The waves whisper jokes that tickle the shore,
While crickets play in a comedic score.
Fireflies flicker, they dance and tease,
And I ignited a laugh with a sneeze in the breeze.

Coastal Reveries at Dusk

As the sun dips low, skies turn to mauve,
I spot a fish that's wearing a hat, what a trove!
Shells scatter secrets, they giggle and jive,
While I tell a joke to a starfish that's shy.

The beach blankets toss like leaves in a whirl,
And a wave gives my sandwich a salty twirl.
I sip my drink, but it slips from my hand,
And the mysteries in the waves can't be planned.

Whispered Secrets in the Sand

Footprints trailing, leading nowhere,
I spy a crab with a meddlesome stare.
The flip-flops argue about who's the best,
While the tides gather stories from East to West.

Kites in the sky, they dance like a dream,
A clam sings loud, with a clamorous theme.
Mischief bubbles like foam in the light,
As we gather laughter to wave goodnight!

Seafoam Kisses

Salty tongues and laughter loud,
Seagulls dive, a raucous crowd.
Flip-flops flying, sunscreen spills,
Mermaids giggle, chasing thrills.

Waves roll in, a foamy dance,
Flip-flop pride takes a chance.
Crabs in tuxedos sneer and scuttle,
While kids try to splash in puddles.

The sandcastles lean, the flags flutter,
While shells conspire to tell you, "Shutter!"
Dolphins wink as they swim by,
And sea cucumbers seem to sigh.

Laughter is the tide that turns,
With ice cream cones that spill and churn.
Fish in shades of pink and lime,
All cheer for this silly rhyme!

Reflection in Calm Waters

Mirror ponds and plops abound,
Frogs become the circus sound.
Ducklings dance in playful rows,
While bobbing turtles strike a pose.

Fish in tuxedos swim with flair,
Jumping jacks, without a care.
One flips high, but lands right here,
Splashing me with surprise and cheer.

Reflections wave, they seem to grin,
As I attempt to join in.
My hair a mess, like seaweed's curl,
The water suggests I give it a twirl.

But ripples giggle, their voiceless fun,
Creating laughter that's never done.
Each splash and wave becomes a jest,
In this silly liquid fest!

Windswept Wanderings

Winds weave tales with a cheeky twist,
And hairdos turn into a mist.
Kites soar high, some take a dive,
While beach balls roll and take a drive.

A crab wearing shades strolls by slow,
As if he's got somewhere to go.
The breeze teases all that it finds,
Playing tricks on blurry minds.

Sandy shoes and laughter blend,
Where every drift seeks a good friend.
Seashell phones that make no sound,
Are giggling as they spin around.

But who cares — the essence is clear,
To be whisked away is a thrill to cheer!
So let the zany winds conspire,
To lift our hearts and take us higher!

Tropical Whispers

Beneath the palms, secrets unfold,
With stories that never get old.
The mango trees sway in delight,
While the parrots chat through the night.

Chasing shadows, we run so free,
Tripping over roots is the tea.
Sugarcane giggles, just like me,
As we plunge into the sugar spree.

The sun wears shades — it's quite the sight,
And fruity drinks are our only plight.
Coconuts bounce like balls of fun,
While we try to dodge the sun.

With music light and dancing feet,
We twirl around to the tropical beat.
In this whimsical, sun-soaked land,
Every day is perfectly planned!

The Sway of Time Beneath the Palms

Under leafy crowns they dance,
With a sway that speaks of chance.
Bouncing coconuts drop near,
Time tickles with a cheerful cheer.

Dreamy naps on sandy beds,
While the sun bounces on our heads.
Laughter echoes in the breeze,
As we swat at pesky bees.

Bouncing back like beach balls thrown,
Every giggle brightly shone.
Swaying low, we share a snack,
Wishing time would never slack.

So here we sit, all in a row,
Watching waves with a funny flow.
A memory made, both odd and sweet,
In this little nook where friends all meet.

Mirth Underneath the Sunlit Canopy

Under the shade, we tell tall tales,
Of mighty fish and hidden sails.
With guffaws that echo wide,
As we leap and jump with pride.

Stray coconuts roll by our feet,
We dodge and weave, oh isn't that neat!
Sipping drinks with wild-eyed glee,
Wouldn't trade this for a cup of tea.

Sun-kissed skin and laughter bright,
We mingle with the playful light.
With every joke, a wave of fun,
Life's a game, and we've just begun.

So gather round for one last throw,
A splash, a laugh, a cheerful show.
With each soft breeze, we raise a cheer,
Here's to fun times, and good friends near!

Footprints in the Sands of Time

Little tracks in golden grains,
Marking all our silly chains.
Running wild as seagulls shout,
Guessing where we'll sprint about.

With every wave, our footprints fade,
Like our plans that never stayed.
Tumbles and turns in the sun,
Who knew having fun was this fun?

Building castles with shaky walls,
Dodging splashes, riding falls.
With a wink and playful tease,
We find delight in every breeze.

So let's make friends with silly tides,
And go where whimsy joyfully rides.
In every step, laughter we entwine,
Painting paths that jestful shine.

A Tapestry of Turquoise and Green

Within these colors, mishaps reign,
Fish in shades of wacky strain.
We ponder life in vibrant spins,
Wondering where the fun begins.

Salty hair and sticky snacks,
As we tiptoe around the cracks.
With every splash, a giggle bursts,
The fun continues, it just thirsts.

Swaying in the lazy sun,
Chasing friends is simply fun.
With every flip and twist around,
In every giggle, pure joy's found.

So here we laugh and happily play,
In a world that would surely sway.
With every shade of ocean's glow,
We find the joy in ebb and flow.

Salt-Sprayed Serenity

A seagull stole my sandwich, oh what a sight,
He squawked with glee, it gave quite a fright.
I waved my arms, I tried to shout,
But he just laughed and flew about.

The sunbathers giggled, sipping their drinks,
While sandy toes wiggled, nobody thinks.
I chased that bird, with all my might,
He whizzed past a sun hat, what a flight!

In the quiet, kids splashed, having such fun,
While I plotted revenge on that mischievous one.
A water balloon, oh what a scheme,
But I ended up wet, it was just a dream!

So if you're at the beach, take heed of this tale,
Don't challenge a bird; you'll surely fail.
Grab your own lunch, and laugh with the rest,
But leave the sandwiches in the cooler; that's best!

Dancing Leaves by the Shore

The palms are prancing, swaying so low,
A dance-off starting; who put on that show?
With each gentle rustle, they twist and they twirl,
While I sip my drink, and give it a whirl.

A crab joined in, with a tiny cha-cha,
Claws outstretched, looked like an eager star.
We all cheered on, 'Go little guy!'
As he danced right past, oh my, oh my!

Next came a pelican, with a silly strut,
He flopped and he flailed, full of pure nut.
The audience roared, the sun shining bright,
This beachside party felt perfectly right!

As day turned to night, and stars filled the sky,
The leaves kept on dancing as I waved goodbye.
Tomorrow again, I'll join the parade,
For a laugh and a jig, in the sun's warm shade!

Breezy Hues of Paradise

A striped umbrella flipped, grabbed by the zephyr,
Taking a stroll like it's out for a venture.
I chased it down, tripping on sand,
It giggled at me, just couldn't understand!

The beach ball bounced past, oh what a sight,
It danced with the waves, caught in pure flight.
I lunged and I leaped, like an acrobat,
But all I caught was a ray of the sunhat!

Towels were flying, like kites in the air,
Kids giggled and squealed, no worry or care.
As I juggled my snacks with one little fling,
I ended up sharing with the gulls on the wing.

With laughter and mess, we all became friends,
In this vibrant chaos, the fun never ends.
So grab your towel, your snacks, and your cheer,
Let's make some memories, let's have some fun here!

Tropic Tales Beneath the Palm

Under the palms, stories do flow,
Of sunscreen mischief and waves that glow.
One lad said he surfed, oh what a feat!
But really he splashed, and landed in feet!

Sandy toes twinkled, like jewels on the shore,
As I told them the tale of a crab wanting more.
He snatched a fish snack, made quite a mess,
We laughed till we cried, I must confess!

A hammock nearby swung gently with ease,
While I napped for a bit, serenaded by bees.
But who would have guessed, in that sunny embrace,
A squirrel swooped in, stole my last ace!

So if you're out playing in sun's warm delight,
Watch out for the critters that roam day and night.
With tales to be shared, let memories flow,
Beneath those grand fronds, where laughter can grow!

Calm Currents and Fragrant Fronds

In the shade where squirrels play,
A coconut falls, what a day!
I dodge it quick, oh what a feat,
That nutty gift could end in defeat.

Seagulls squawk as I sip my drink,
While pondering life on the brink.
They steal my fries without a care,
I glare at them, just a glare of despair.

The breeze whispers stories of yore,
Of sunburns and sand, and much, much more.
I laugh while I watch a child trip,
Right into the sand with a glorious flip.

So here I bask, in laughter's embrace,
With nature's antics, I keep pace.
Nothing is better than this delight,
Even if it means I'll fall at night.

Celestial Hues Over Water

The sky's painted pink and blue,
As tourists argue, 'What's that brew?'
They sip their drinks with silly smiles,
While I perfect my beachy styles.

A crab scuttles with style and flair,
Stealing shells with a brave air.
I try to catch his sneaky twitch,
But he tugs away, like a clever witch.

The sun sets low, it's time to feast,
With funny hats, we're quite the beast.
Laughter rolls like waves on shore,
We're all just friends, who could want more?

A seagull joins our merry band,
Our party's wild and very unplanned.
It's a comedy, life's a funny chase,
With messy hair and goofy grace.

Palms and Poetry

A poet stands with ink-stained hands,
Complaining about strict lunch plans.
He scribbles rhymes on a paper plate,
While seagulls circle, oh what a fate!

With palms swaying to the beat,
I feel the rhythm beneath my feet.
A dance-off starts, it's all in fun,
With crabs as judges, and the crowd's just begun.

The laughter echoes, a sunny tune,
As everyone joins under the moon.
I trip and tumble into the sand,
But the silly crabs all give a hand.

So here we sit, with hearts so light,
Each goofy moment, pure delight.
In a world of jests, life's a spree,
Where palms sway gently, carefree as can be.

Driftwood Dreams

Amidst the driftwood, tales are spun,
Of clumsy treads and beachy fun.
I spot a flip-flop on a log,
Is it lost or part of the dialogue?

With sand everywhere, I take a stance,
And watch in awe as crabs advance.
They pinch at rhymes and tickle my toes,
While my friends break out with silly prose.

A wave rolls in, oh what a sight,
It drenches all in pure delight.
We squeal and shout and run away,
As water dances, come what may.

So here we dream, in sunlight's glow,
With driftwood dreams, our laughter flows.
Life's a stage where we play and roam,
In our sandy kingdom, we've found our home.

Gentle Embrace of Summer's Breath

The sun's hot, like a frying pan,
And here I am, a beach bum man.
Flip-flops flapping, a goofy sight,
Caught in a wave, oh what a fright!

Seagulls squawk, they steal my chips,
I chase them down with silly flips.
Sandy snacks are lost in the fray,
Next time, I'll eat them all away!

Smart sun hats blown by the breeze,
Look! There's Uncle Joe, he sneezes.
What's that? A tan line shaped like a cloud?
Oh dear, I'll laugh that's legal and loud!

Here comes a wave, big and round,
Socks are soaked, can't save 'em now.
I'll ride this tide, with guts and glee,
My splashy fate, come laugh with me!

Serenity Found in Nature's Heart

Under palm fronds, I'll sip my drink,
With tiny umbrellas, and think, think, think.
The mixer's sweet, but oh, so strong,
I hum the tunes of the tropics' song.

A crab walks by, with swagger and style,
I can't help but grin, it's been a while.
Will he dance? Oh, let's make a bet,
I'll lead the conga, my biggest regret!

With laughter as bright as the sun's own rays,
We'll mimic dolphins in utterly gross ways.
The waves pull us in, oh what a thrill,
With water so cool, a cheeky chill!

Oh, nature's heart, with humor so vast,
Remind me again, can fun really last?
Let's splash and twirl, no cares in sight,
We'll dance through the day, into the night!

Flickers of Twilight on the Shore

As twinkling stars begin their show,
I trip on sand, and there I go!
A tumble so graceful, like a new dance craze,
Nature's applause for my hilarious ways.

The sun waves goodbye with a purple flair,
And the beach ball flies, oh, into the air!
Catch me if you can, I shout with glee,
But it's Uncle Dan, who fell in a tree!

We gather around with stories to tell,
Like ghosts of the beach, we laugh, oh so well.
A serenade of shrimp and fishy fables,
We feast and chuckle, eating with labels.

The moon's glow is bright, a spotlight on me,
For a grand finale, all quite silly.
With flip-flop rhythms, we dance till we drop,
In this twilight bliss, it's a laugh-fueled hop!

Colors of Dawn in the Tropics

Dawn breaks in hues of pink and gold,
I spill my coffee, feeling bold.
The sun kicks in, the day begins,
As splashes of color lead to grins.

Birds are chirping a funky tune,
I think they're singing at the moon.
What's that? A squirrel with flair and style,
He's shaking his tail, and staying awhile!

The beach is waking, oh what a scene,
I slip on sunscreen, looking like green.
With sandy toes and picnic treats,
It's time for laughter, and sunny beats!

So raise your glass, let's make a cheer,
For colors and giggles with no fear.
In the bright of the morn, let's run free,
And dance to the rhythm, just you and me!

www.ingramcontent.com/pod-product-compliance
Lightning Source LLC
Chambersburg PA
CBHW072222070526
44585CB00015B/1456